MOMENTS MATTER

A Moment that Truly Mattered to Me

Amarie Riley
Asiah Thorpe
Avery Johnson
Cara Akin
Deana Akin
Isabella Patricia Sanchez
Jillian Blackwell
Julie Robinson
Sophia Do
William Monroe
Wizdom Monroe

BK
ROYSTON
Publishing

BK Royston Publishing
P. O. Box 4321
Jeffersonville, IN 47131
502-802-5385
http://www.bkroystonpublishing.com
bkroystonpublishing@gmail.com

© Copyright – 2017

Cover Design: Kamaal Designs

ISBN: 978-1-946111-43-2

Printed in the United States of America

MOMENTS MATTER
MISSION AND MOTTOS

Dedicated to Educating and Empowering Youth. Moments Matter Incorporated was created to allow our youth to experience moments that they may not otherwise experience. Our team consists of educators and facilitators who have devoted their time and life to the growth and development of our youth. We truly believe that when they know better, that they can now do better. Our events have not only left lasting moments in the lives of our participants, but also allowed them to understand that every moment that they experience good or bad matters.

GIRLS MOTTO: I am Intelligent, healthy, Caring, Loving and Beautiful. I will not allow the moment to define me!! I will define the moment!!!

BOYS MOTTO: I am Intelligent, Healthy, Caring, Love and Handsome. I will not allow the moment to define me!! I will define the moment!!!

TABLE OF CONTENTS

AMARIE'S

MOMENT

My Moment That Matters

By: Amarie Riley

I am 12 years old and I attend Ramsey middle school. I am an only child, and I live with just my mom. But recently, I have been specifically seeing my dad. At this time, it was just me and my mom. My mom did everything for me and me only.

At this time, I was 8 years old. I hadn't seen my dad in about a year. Since me and my dad were so close, I got really disappointed and sad when I thought about him. Mom and I were staying at a friend's house during a wind storm. After my mom told me good night, I saw my friend and his dad telling each other good night. It made me remember when I used to tell my dad good night.

To better express myself, I started to cry. I walked to my mom and asked her, "Why haven't we seen dad?" The reason why I was upset was, because I was worried and upset that I couldn't see him in person. So Mom and I talked about how I can see him at any time until I calmed down. About a week later, my mom surprised me. We went through a neighborhood that was not familiar to me. That's when I saw my dad siting on the edge of the porch waiting. I ran towards him almost starting to cry. It was awesome when I could talk to him and check up on him; telling him I missed him. I was so excited.

Since that day, I have become much closer with my dad. Talking to him on the phone is more often now. He takes me to get my haircut on the weekends or on special days. I have been more appreciative of the moments that I spend with him. I love my dad. He tells me that too every time he comes. He will always be there for me any time he can. Even though he and my mom aren't together, they would get back together just for me. For kids out there who can't see their family, because something happened to that special someone; like they are dead or in jail. Just remember this. They did everything for you. They may be gone, but they did everything for you. They still love you. They still care for you. I know that you are worried about them, but someone on this earth cares for you. So it is ok.

ASIAH'S

MOMENT

The moment that mattered the most to me was.............

The day my stepdad adopted me.

By: Asiah Thorpe

Before he adopted me and got married to my mom, life was hard. I didn't have a father figure besides my grandpa (on my mom's side). My biological father didn't care about me or my sister. He didn't care if something bad happened to us. It felt like I had a hole in my heart where he should have been. After years of my mom and biological father arguing, they finally got divorced. Many months later, my mom met my soon to be stepdad. I was very young when I met him. I was scared of him, but he was nice to me. I wouldn't let him touch me. But after weeks, I got used to him and let him play with me. He would buy me dolls, and we would watch TV.

They dated for about 8-9 months. It took me 4 months to get used to him. It took my sister 10 weeks to get used to him. We would make him cards saying that we loved him and that he was funny. He would hang up our cards or keep them in my parent's room. Then if he had a day off; while we were at school, he would make cards saying he loves us too and place them in our drawers.

I don't remember the proposal, but I was a flower girl at the wedding. My god mom had to hold me, because I was squirming wanting to run up and hug all my family members.

They got married April 7, 2012. All was good. My sister and I loved him a lot. I finally had filled the space in my heart where my biological father should have been. He loved us no matter what. Even though he wasn't my blood, I loved him until my world came crashing down.

First my cousin; Essence Martin, had a heart attack. She went to the hospital. And on the operation table, she had another heart attack. She died at the age of 29. It devastated me very much, because she was my favorite cousin. At the practice funeral, I couldn't take in the fact that she was gone. I cried the entire time. 1 thing I remember about her was I called her cousin Pete. The next day, I went to a cousin's house while the funeral was going on. 2 years later, my grandpa; Curtis Montgomery died. It felt like all was lost; like my heart kept getting dented over and over again. I still remember them, but I know I have to let them go.

3 years later, my family is living happily. Until one day, my mom brings up the topic of changing mine and my sister's last name from Hatcher to Thorpe. It required us to get a lawyer, get our biological father to sign something (which he refused to sign) and to go to court. After he refused to sign the paper, we talked to our lawyer and we still got to change our last names. We went court June 20, 2017. We made it official and had a party at Roosters. We both got stuffed animals (I got a Donald Duck tsumtsum, and my sister got a frog, she named it Frog Marley). We got pictures with the judge and our lawyer. We were now part of the Thorpe family. My family has had a history. I have 2 dads, but only 1 loves me. When I have school events and my family comes my friends

ask, "Where is your real dad?" But always my answer is, "Right here."

Don't let anyone tell you who and what your family should look like. It is your family. You love who you love.

Many years and months later, I remembered all the things I went through just so my mom could be happy and my sister and I could be safe and be with someone who loves us. So if I have 1 thing to say it's, "I love you dad, and you love me." And that is the moment that matters to me, what yours?

-Nyasiah (Asiah) Thorpe

AVERY'S

MOMENT

My Dad and I

By: Avery Johnson

I met my dad at the age 10 after 7 years. I was so excited to meet him after such a long time. When I first met him I was nervous, but I was excited too (mixed emotions). So, here's my story.

I started noticing I never said, "Daddy." It was always Mommy, Mommy and Mommy. Then I noticed that when I went to practice, the movies and to school, there were other kids around me they had a 'Daddy.' I was confused. I wanted a Daddy, and I wanted a Daddy now. In second grade, I got to make a wish list of three items. One of the items was that I would like to meet up with my dad. I took it home to show my mom, and she asked me did I really want to meet up with him. I said no, but I really wanted to in my mind. From then on, I kept thinking about it. Then, I finally told her that I really did want to meet up with my dad and she said, "Ok."

Three years later, something happened that got me a step closer to meeting my dad.

I was talking with my counselor that helped me with life issues. He asked if it was ok if my mom came in to talk also, I said that was fine. We all started talking and my Mom said, "So I was working the other day, and your dad came in to ask about you." "Hold on. Hold on one second, what did you say?" "Your dad wants to meet back up with you," She said. "For the first time in 7 long years, I was meeting up with my dad," I said. I asked my counselor if he knew about it and he said, "Yes." OH MY GOSH! I was so excited.

They told me that I was going to get to meet up with him. OH MY GOSH! My brain was telling me to jump up and down in excitement.

A few weeks later, the day finally came. I was so happy. I was just a little bit nervous from the time I woke up that morning. I picked out an outfit. I really did not care what I wore. I was just too excited to care about an outfit. I just threw something on that matched. I ran out the door in excitement, and I waited for my mom in the car. And when we got going, I just wanted to jump up and down in excitement.

When we arrived at the restaurant, he was waiting for me outside the door. I had mixed emotions. I was mostly happy, but also a little bit nervous. It smelled like fresh rolls and steak. So then I went inside with him, and we ordered our food. We found a spot to sit down, and we talked about all of the things going on in our lives.

When it was time to leave, I didn't want to go home. I was hoping I could spend more time with him, but I was so happy I got to see him. I gave him a big hug. We said bye to each other, then he had to go. When my mom picked me up, I told her about it. Again I wanted to jump up and down. I was thinking that night about our time. It felt like the best time in my whole life.

The End

CARA'S

MOMENT

MOMENTS MATTER

My Birthday Weekend Adventure

BY: Cara Akin

Hi, my name is Cara, and I am the oldest child in a family of four. I have my mom, dad, and sister named Deanna, who is also writing this book. She is the most EVIL being you'll meet; although, she usually hides this behind an innocent facade. Anyways, I am currently fourteen and in the eighth grade. I enjoy writing, reading, piano, science, school, tennis and makeup. My current obsession is Hamilton, Riverdale, and the periodic table of elements. That's all about me; so without further ado, here's my moment that mattered to me.

I stretched and yawned as I dreaded getting up this the morning; when suddenly, I remembered today was the day I was going to my cousin's house to celebrate my 14th birthday! I got dressed quick as a flash, then I ran out to get breakfast when I realized it was only 7:00 am. Groaning softly, I grabbed my bags and settled down on the couch with a book until my parents were ready to leave.

Finally, at 10:00 A.M it was time to go. I threw my bags in the car with a thud, and we were off. As the GPS chimed, "You have reached your destination on left." I was shaking with excitement, even though we were meeting at a McDonald's in the middle of nowhere. As we pulled into the parking lot, we saw my cousin, Brittany's mom's red SUV. We waited for my aunt and my cousin Ashley to arrive, so we could start our weekend adventure.

Finally after what felt like HOURS, my aunt pulled up. Brittany and I grabbed our stuff and got in my aunt's car whilst desperately trying to avoid my mom's over exaggerated hugs coming my way. After the adults finished chatting, we were off on our first adventure of the weekend. During the hour long trip there, we decided to go to the mall first. We turned up the radio all the way and sang loudly all the way there.

As we pulled into the mall parking lot and parked, my aunt gave me half the money my mom had given me to spend over the course of the weekend. She kept the other half for safe keeping. We were bouncing all in our seats full of excitement, because we would be on our own without an adult following us and watching our every move for the very first time. Before my aunt could even finish speaking about how we needed to stay together while she was shopping on her own and to be back at a certain time, we slammed the car doors and left my aunt in the dust as we ran through the J.C Penney entrance commenting on the cute outfits we saw on the way in.

By the time we got to the escalators in the middle of the mall, we were panting and out of breath as we rode up to the second floor. When we got to the top we debated on where to go when we saw it, 'PINK NATION!' We all looked to each other and silently made a group agreement to go in and shop till we dropped!

As we walked in, Ashley went straight to the leggings, Brittany to the perfumes and me to the shirts, and we were lost in our own worlds. Thirty minutes later, we walked out of Pink Nation with two bags of merchandise: Brittany with perfume, and Ashley with too much stuff to keep track of.

Knowing Ashley and Brittany, I knew they would fly through the money they were given by their parents. I; of course, would rather spend my money somewhere LESS expensive in the mall.

Next, we planned out the rest of our day at the mall. It consisted of going to Rue 21, Forever 21, H&M and Charlotte Russe. We walked into Rue 21, and we all three made a beeline for the cute ripped jeans over in the corner causing Brittany to drop her Pink Nation bag (no merchandise was damaged.)

Laughing, we went through the jeans all picking out one to try on. Then we went over to the shirts, where I picked out a cute striped long sleeve shirt with the shoulders cut out. We were all really surprised at how cute it was. So when we saw a dress on the way to the fitting rooms with the same pattern, we all had to try one on. The line was a MILE long. So during the wait, we grabbed some DOLLAR chokers to try on. Yes you read correctly, DOLLAR chokers!

Finally, three fitting rooms were opened at once. So we each followed a sales attendant to one, and we set our merchandise from Pink Nation down on the ground and got changed. I remember I got butterflies in my stomach when I realized I had been in there for nearly FIFTEEN MINUTES. Then I heard both of them yell my name, so I stepped out in my striped dress to say my opinion on their outfits when I realized we were all wearing the same thing! We all felt like little kids again dressing up like we did many years ago.

We all laughed realizing how similar we were as we went back into our rooms to put our own clothes back on and grab our merchandise from Pink Nation. Fifteen minutes later, we were on our way to Forever 21 with three new bags of merchandise. Brittany with a shirt, Ashley with a dress and a choker, and me with ripped jeans, a dress, a choker and a shirt.

On the way to Forever 21, we passed Aeropostale with neon lights screaming 'CLEARANCE SALE, 50% OFF ON ALL JEANS AND JEGGINGS!' We were super excited, because so far everywhere we had gone was much too expensive for a bunch of teenagers with a limited amount of money, even though my cousin's spending methods were MUCH different than mine. So we veered to the left and into the store in search of some good deals, when we realized that their so called sale of 50% off was still $30 or $40. We walked out of that place as fast as we could go, before a sales attendant could catch up to us and use their magic to make us buy something we didn't really want.

We were all feeling a little bit disappointed by this time, but when we walked into H&M we were expecting better things. We were sad to see that H&M only had a little bit more on sale than Aeropostale. I ended up buying a pair of red high waisted skinny jeans. What made matters even worse is that we only had one hour left to shop!

By this time, we weren't expecting much from Charlotte Russe, but boy were we wrong! This was the best place yet! Everything was so extravagantly set up and the sales attendants were so kind. We roamed around for a little bit, and then we spotted the shoes...... these were the type of shoes you see in your crazy Instagram feed and you wonder why on earth would anyone buy these?! They were red thigh high heeled boots. Ashley being well… Ashley had to try them on.

Let's just say, they were a pain to put on and a pain to take off too as the sales attendant who had to come help us soon found out. We saw tons of cute clothes, and we raced each other to the fitting rooms and took tons of pictures of ourselves in these new cute outfits we had picked out. But sadly, by this time the awesome sales weren't even low enough to save us. We were out of money.

We had fifteen minutes left by this time, and we debated on whether going ahead and meeting my aunt was a direction we should head in. When finally, we all saw the place where you can get samples galore… no not Teavana, SEPHORA!

We rushed in like our life depended on it. Brittany and Ashley put on a full face of makeup with samples, while I got my color IQ and my second sample of foundation. I remember Ashley looked at her phone, and her mom had texted her saying that it was time to go meet up TWENTY MINUTES AGO!!

We thanked the workers that had assisted us, and we ran out of the store and down the escalators catching sight of my aunt checking the time for probably the hundredth time this hour. We got off of the elevators with me almost falling to my death, as we rushed down them and ran to catch up with my aunt as she began the long walk to the car. We all started talking at once about all the cute clothes we got, and my aunt could probably tell it was going to be a long day.

My aunt backs up and asks us where we want to go to eat, and we all reply "CHICK-FIL-A!" My aunt laughs as we do so, and says that we are all so much alike. We nod agreeing as we pull into the Chick-fil-a parking lot.

We all jump out of the car and walk inside like civilized human beings for once. We get in line behind TONS of people, and I look around in awe as a waiter comes up to us with a high tech tablet and takes our order. Finally; after what feels like hours, we are at the cash register where they give us our drinks at this futuristic Chick-fil-a and a table marker as well.

We look around in surprise. We realized that the only table open is a HUGE table, and no one wants to sit outside in the freezing weather we now call 'Fall.' So we grab our condiments and sit down.

Finally, after a long wait we get our food and dig in, when a lady comes up and asks if we would switch tables with her since she had a larger group that couldn't all squeeze into a small table. We of course agreed, switched with her, got settled in and kept eating.

A few minutes later, the same lady comes up with a bag of cookies she bought for us and thanks us again and again. We are touched by her kindness. We thank her again and again and take the cookies graciously since we're not the kind of people to turn down free food. About ten minutes later, we are back in the car again and on the way to my aunt's house.

Finally after a long day of shopping at the mall and 50% off disappointments, we finally pull into my aunt's driveway. We grab our merchandise, our bags and we walk in the back door and are greeted by the friendly licks of my aunt's dogs Oscar and Max.

We bring our stuff up to Ashley's room, throw it in the corner, change into our new outfits, touch up our makeup and we run back downstairs to pick up Ashley's friend and go to the county fair.

Twenty minutes later, we pull onto the muddy ground with Ashley's friend sandwiched between us. I peeled myself off the seat and am greeted by a blast of icy cold wind when I open my door. Ashley's friend comes out behind me, followed by Brittany. The door is slammed closed, and we're out in the cold.

We run into the fair panicking, because we thought of everyone. Ashley was going to hang out with us and introduce us to our 'would already be on rides,' but then we find out the rides don't open for another THIRTY MINUTES!!

While we wait those long thirty minutes, we buy a HUGE bucket of French fries to share and we each buy a BIG lemonade. We sit down at a picnic table, and all of our face's pucker at once as we take a big sip of it. It was DISGUSTING and SOUR. We soon found out why, as Ashley's friend opened hers and pulled out HALF OF A LEMON from the bottom. YUCK! Luckily by that time, we throw away our lemonades and the rides are opening.

We race to the Starship ride, and I have butterflies in my stomach as the lights go off and the red blinking lights flash on and off. Then it starts spinning faster, faster and faster, and all the kids on the ride start pushing off the ground causing their panels to slide up and down. Brittany and I look at each other in awe, as one guy stands horizontal as the speed increases until finally he almost falls when the ride slows down.

As we all stumble off of the ride in a single line, Brittany and I are in awe, and Brittany looks sick until Ashley's friends throws up. Then Brittany looks healthy as can be compared to her. We buy Ashley's friend a cool drink, and we sit with her for several minutes until she looks normal again. Next, we join a big group of Ashley's friends, and we go to the petting zoo.

The first thing that hits me is the smell, but then the sight of cute little rabbits. But for Ashley; on the other hand, the first thing that hits her is a donkey; an ugly muddy donkey. She starts crying about it, because she thinks it's so cute. Brittany thinks it's cute too, but all I see a muddy mammal that hasn't had a bath in far too long.

We leave behind the cute bunnies and the stinky donkey and follow the crowd. We cut through this small path for horses not thinking there might actually be horses on it. That's when the scariest moment of the night happens, a lady on a BIG brown horse rides by saying, "Sorry guys he got spooked by something." By this time, everyone is across, but Brittany. We are all frozen in horror and shock as Brittany almost gets trampled by the horse, and the group lets out an audible sigh of relief as Brittany makes it across in one piece.

That's when we see my aunt, and she see us. We debate running, but then I see that Jacquelyn; their next door neighbor and a close friend of mine, is with her. So I walk in that direction so Ashley and Brittany have no choice but to follow me.

Jacquelyn and I exchange hugs and conversation, and I introduce her to Brittany. Jacquelyn and I catch up since we haven't talked for months, as we walk to the next ride. When we get to the next ride, Jacquelyn catches sight of her friends from band camp and runs off with them.

We wait in the hour long line. But sadly right when it's our turn, all the rides close and the fair was over. We run back to my aunt, and we get back in the car with three more people than we came with and drive around to each of Ashley's friend's houses to drop them off.

By the time we get back to my aunt's house, we're all disappointed at how the fair turned out. As we walk in Ashley's room and catch sight of the food and Doctor Pepper, everything is looking all right again.

We all flop down on Ashley's bed and decide on doing makeovers. So we do a full on glam look, and spend fifteen minutes posting picture of us on Snapchat. Next, we ate our chips. Who doesn't love food?

Now this is where things got crazy.... So, we bought some Mountain Dews for Brittany, since Ashley and I aren't allowed to drink them because we get hyper so we thought *one small sip won't hurt anyone.* WRONG!!!! I talked loud and laughed at EVERYTHING for no reason whatsoever, and Ashley just got CRAZY! Even more crazy than usual. After that sugar rush though, we were all knocked out for the rest of the night which was probably a relief for my poor aunt.

The next day around noon, we wake up still groggy from the night before. We get dressed in our newly bought clothes, and go downstairs when we all realize with a wave of sadness that it's our last day here. Then my mom, dad, sister, Grammy and Grampy get here for the party and everything was looking up again.

I give hugs to everyone. Then my mom tells us that she forgot that they would have my sister's new loft bed in the car, so there wouldn't be enough room for all of us in her car. So Brittany and I would be staying one more day. After this great news Ashley, Brittany and I all had a moment of teenage girl happiness and then it's time for cake!

I'm surrounded by happiness and songs as I blow out my fourteen candles, and then just like that it's time to say goodbye. My grandparents would be going home, and my mom would be hanging out with my aunt and to younger cousins. I give big hugs to everyone especially my parents for the extra day I got to spend with my cousins.

My dad tells us that in about thirty minutes, we would be going to the Levy with him and my sister Deanna. The Levy is basically Fourth Street Live. We all nod and yell that we're getting ready, as we run up the stairs to change again and do our makeup. Thirty minutes later with newly rejuvenated glowy skin, we hop in the car and drive about thirty long minutes there.

We walk with my dad to the front of the main building where he tells to stay together and what time we need to be back, and then we're off. We go into Barnes and Noble in hope of finding a Starbucks, but there's no Starbucks to be found. We walk inside of the main building and glance longingly at the stuff in the windows we can't afford.

On our way out, we see a spa where fish eat off your dead skin and we run out of there as fast as we can. Next, we're out in the humid weather again as we climb a HUGE grassy hill to the place where all the vendors are.

We meet up with another one of Ashley's friends, and we all get Sprites to quench our thirst. We walk around a bit longer when we realize we're LATE. I groan silently as I realize that the entrance is a LONG way back. When I look back the other way, all of them were climbing up the same HUGE hill only this side was full of ROCKS!

They climb up that with the ease of a spider monkey, while I struggle almost falling to my death a couple of times until finally we make it out...... at a busy intersection. I groan wondering why we have such bad luck as we run down the hill and across the intersection until we get back to the Levy area.

We ran, ran and ran until we find my dad who has been waiting for a while. As we walk back to the car, he gives us a big talk about staying together which we didn't always do. We get to the car and drives to BW3's while my dad continues to speak. After he's done, Ashley passes us a note on her nice IPhone apologizing for running off with her friend, and thanking us for not ratting her out. Brittany and I reply back, "That's what friends are for."

We get to BW 3's after a tough time of finding it. We get in and the waitress says there isn't enough room even, though she lets the people behind us in. They have the same amount of people which puzzles us all quite a bit, so we leave. We find another BW3's, and we're seated by our waitress who gives us our drinks. The food takes what feels like hours to get there, even though in reality it's only about fifteen minutes.

The food finally arrives after a long wait, and we dig in like we haven't eaten for days. About thirty minutes later, we all finish and we are super-duper stuffed. We drive back to my aunt's house, and we all go up to Ashley's room where we all lay back exhausted. After we are well rested, we do one last makeover, make funny videos and we all fall asleep in our clothes.

We rise bright and early which is really one P.M; but for me on a weekend, that's early. My aunt smiles as we're FINALLY awake, and she says it's time to drop me and Brittany off. We throw all our stuff in the car, and we prepare for the hour long drive by turning the music up. We drive back to the McDonald's whilst singing the whole way.

We get back to the McDonalds in the middle of nowhere, and we're slightly disappointed as we spot Brittany's mom's S.U.V and my dad's car. Brittany and I both know its past time for us to leave.

The adults chat for a while, then we exchange hugs and say goodbye. My dad and I decide to go see the locked dam that is nearby. We see that and it really cool except, I have to navigate through mud in heels and a nice dress (YIKES!) But for the fun I had and the stronger bonds I formed with my cousins, ruining that dress could have been worth it!

On the hour long drive back to our house, my dad asks me about my weekend and I tell him. By the end of my story, my eyelids are heavy and we're back home. I stagger inside exhausted, and I go straight to my bedroom avoiding my mom's questions as I fall asleep.

Around 6 P.M, I wake up slightly confused as I realize it's not morning yet. I yawn loudly and climb out of bed and stagger into the kitchen to make myself some cereal. Why not have cereal for dinner?

I tell my mom about everything we did. We laugh together when I tell her about the incident of the thigh high, high heeled boots. She is in shock when I tell her the amusing story of the lemonade with half a lemon at the bottom. I remember. She said from what I told her, we must have formed some pretty strong bonds together, I replied, "We definitely did."

DEANNA'S

MOMENT

MOMENTS MATTER

Sokka the Cat-Dog

By Deanna Akin

I am the youngest of our family of four. I have a mom, dad, and a VERY annoying sister, who is actually also writing in this book. Actually, we have a family of 6, because I always count my pets. We have two pets; both are cats, Digit and Sokka. This story is actually about how I got Sokka. I am also 11 and in the 5th grade, and I have just started Middle School in the biggest middle school in Indiana! Yay. If you cannot tell after reading this, my hobbies are: annoying my sister; Cara, eating Chick-fil-A, playing Roblox, googling "black and white cats" to see Sokka lookalikes and hanging with my Sokka Baby! Enjoy!

It was May 28th, 2016, at 9:00 am. We were driving to the vet, because our dog Millie had cancer in her leg, and we found out too late. When the doctor called us in, my mom was crying. I cried a little too. The vet gave her a shot to make her sleep, and she fell asleep right on my foot! We left the room before the doctor gave her the shot that would make her die.

After she was put down, we drove to the nearby J.B. Ogle Animal Center. We had already looked at their website, and found a cat that we liked named Katie. When we got there and found her, we didn't really like her. We looked at other cats, but none of them really fit what we wanted. My dad wanted a cat that would cuddle with him, and my mom wanted a shorthair cat that was not declawed.

We found a cage that had two tuxedo cats. One was a longhair and one was a shorthair. We got the shorthair out (his name was Ned), then went into the cat room. He had all black fur except for the middle of his face, his chest and his paws. His paws were HUGE! His pupils were so big that made his entire eyes were black. He immediately went under the other cages in the room. I managed to lure him out with a toy, and we held him. He would literally just sit in your arms. He was also a shorthair so he fit our needs, but we completely forgot to check if he was declawed. We just thought he was nice and wouldn't show his claws. When my mom held him she said, "Sokka! That's what he is, a Sokka!" She got that name from Avatar; the Last Airbender, because the character named Sokka was a kind, clumsy guy. The name stuck (my dad was not happy about that. Apparently, he's never named ANY of the 5 animals we've had).

We put Sokka back into his cage, and then went outside to talk about it. It was a SUPER hot day (for me, I get hot easily), and I wanted to go into somewhere air conditioned; even if it was the car. They told me that they were either going to get Sokka, or we were going to another shelter. I started crying because I wanted Katie, but neither my dad nor mom wanted her. We settled on going to the New Albany Animal Shelter just to look. We had got our other cat Digit there, but he is scared of everything and fat, so I wasn't expecting much.

We went out to Taco Bell and ate. Now, my favorite restaurant is Chick-fil-A. Back then I couldn't eat much there because of my food allergies (I was allergic to milk, wheat, pork, and eggs), so we went to Taco Bell. Then we drove off in our car.

We arrived at the New Albany shelter, but didn't find any cats we liked. We left and we realized I had left my purse at Taco Bell (like I said, I had food allergies then, so I had to have an Epipen with me at all times), so we had to drive back there.

After that, we drove back to the J.B. Ogle Center and adopted Sokka. We drove home and let him out in the garage, and we found out he was declawed, so we had to keep him inside because he couldn't defend himself. We had to keep him in the garage for a while, so Digit could smell him through the door and be prepared.

I slowly grew more and more attached to Sokka, and I felt so bad when he was mewing and banging on the door to be let out. Every day I would wake up at 6, run downstairs and throw the door open. Then Sokka and I would have a race up the stairs. He was only 1, so he would always try to attack Digit. Digit hated it, but I thought it was funny. Actually, I still do...

Fast forward about 2 months. Sokka was allowed out of the garage, and my parents said he could sleep with me. Sokka's personality was finally starting to shine through. He did this little thing that I call barking, but it doesn't sound like a dog bark. It's like a faint scratchy meow, and he does it when he sees a moth, a squirrel, a bunny or anything like that. He also LOVES going outside. I bought him a blue harness with a leash, so he could go outside safely, and I saved up for it by starting a dog walking business. So, of course, he knew his mommy could do better than a leash, and it didn't turn out too well. He would just lay on the ground and he wouldn't move. He also does this thing, which I call 'him giving you a kiss.' He doesn't actually lick you, he just head-butts you with his nose. It the cutest and nicest thing EVER!!! Well, he IS the cutest and nicest thing in the universe, so, yeah.

About 7 months later, I got an idea to get Sokka a cat stroller. I researched them and found that the best quality; but also not too expensive, was an OxGord stroller. I got a plain black one (because the colors were more money) and waited for it to arrive. When it did, I put Sokka in it, zipped it up, and drove him around. He absolutely LOVED it, and he still does.

About one month ago in October, we re-did me and my sister's rooms. We each got a budget to spend for our rooms. I got a loft bed with a desk under it and some other stuff. I had to lift Sokka up to the bed for him to sleep with me, and I always worried he would hurt his paws when he jumped down (it didn't help; he wouldn't let anyone help him down). So I used the last of my budget to buy him step things. There are three things: a base where he can lay and two shelves he can jump on. The base and shelves have fake leaves that form a wall around the shelves so he feels like he's outside.

To this day, I still spoil and pamper him. Sokka is basically my glue. If I didn't have him, I would fall apart. I also still do everything I can for the J.B. Ogle Center. (http://www.jbogleanimalshelter.com/) I volunteer there, I recommend people to give them donations in my class newspaper I run, and I gave my Girl Scout leader the idea of our troop volunteering there for a day. So this was a moment that truly mattered.

Sokka has done many hilarious things. One of them is: he will fetch things (he really thinks he's a dog). He loves pipe cleaners and string, and one day I got the idea to tie a bell to a pipe cleaner. It is his FAVORITE toy. So I will fake throw it 3 times, then throw it and he chases after it. Then he'll pick it up in his mouth and run back to where I am. Then he drops it at my feet and meows until I pick it up.

Another funny thing he's done is: we have a refrigerator that has an ice machine, and it makes a sound when you're getting ice, so Sokka runs in. He loves ice for some odd reason. So one day, I gave him an ice cube, and I sild it across our wood floor. Well, he picked it up in his mouth and brought it back to me, but when he tried to set it down, it got stuck to the side of his mouth! It was just hanging there, but he couldn't get it off! So I had to pull it off. It was so funny, and I got it on video!

The third funny thing he's done is with Digit. They always fight and sometimes it's funny, but this time was SO hilarious. We have his cat stand thing, and it has 3 stories, each has a hole in the front to get into. So Sokka was on the top (which he likes, because he's out in the open), and Digit was on the bottom tier. Digit is stupid. So he was batting at Sokka's tail, and Sokka got annoyed. Sokka took his paw (which is giant compared to Digit's) and whacked him in the face. Digit recoiled, but then Sokka jumped down off the floor... RIGHT ONTO DIGIT!! Digit freaked out and did his ugly lemur meow (lemurs have these weird.... screams, I guess), and I started laughing so hard. Then Sokka jumped onto the table I was sitting at, and gave me one of his 'kisses.'

The most recent thing he's done is: run away. Yep. So, he loves going outside and sometimes I just let him out, follow him and watch him (that sounds really creepy). He always bolts out the door. So he did that, and he went into these bushes into my house. They are really big, but I can never go into them. So, I ran to catch him before he went so far I can't get him. I ran into one of those bushes that all the thorns get stuck to you, and I had to stop and take out EVERY SINGLE ONE. By the time I got them out and looked up, Sokka was gone. "Why do we even have that bush?" I grumbled as I headed down towards our backyard. I figured he ran into the woods behind our house. I looked into the bushes one more time, he wasn't there. Then I headed towards the woods. I looked around, but didn't see him. THEN I started panicking. I looked in and around the bushes, and then I heard a rustle. I whipped around and saw a glimpse of black & white. I ran down the hill and saw my Sokka Baby! He saw me and went deeper into the woods. "Oh no, you don't mister!" I said and scooped him up. "Thanks for giving me a heart attack," I said to him while I held on tight to him. "Just for that, you're grounded for 6 weeks!" I told him as we went inside. Actually, that story wasn't really funny. For me it wasn't. My dad thought it was though.

ISABELLA'S

MOMENT

THE DAY MY SISTER WAS BORN

By: Isabella Patricia Sanchez

Have you ever had a special moment that mattered to you? Well I have. When I was 7, I loved drawing, playing with dolls and dressing up. I would dress up by myself and my dolls, but the clothes were too big for my dolls. I had a lot of dolls, and I had played all of them. But something didn't feel right, I was lonely. I have 2 brothers, but they never wanted to play dolls or dress up. Every day it would be the same.

"Hey Paul, wanna play dolls?" I would say.

"No." He would say.

"Hey Angel, wanna play dress up?" I'd say.

"No." He would also say.

I would be in my room playing by myself, and I'd hear my brothers playing together. I would feel so lonely. Then one day I told my mom I wanted a sister. Every day at night, I prayed for a sister.

"Dear Lord, I really want a sister."

And on my 8th birthday I wished for a sister and still no sister, so I prayed more.

"Please lord I really want a sister."

A few weeks later came and still no sister. I was so impatient. So I kept praying. Then came my 9th birthday, and I wished for a sister but no sister.

About a month later I was in my room and my mom said,

"We need to tell you something."

"Ok." My brothers and I said.

"I'm pregnant." My mom said. I froze. I didn't know what to say.

"What!?" I say finally.

I thought this was a joke, but she shows us the pregnancy test. I was so happy, and I was jumping up and down. In my head I was saying, 'A girl! A girl!' I was really hoping for a girl! So, months went by and finally time for the ultra sound to see the baby's gender. My whole family went to the doctor's, and we went in and they took us to a room. Then the doctor rubbed some jelly stuff on my mom's stomach. So as they did the ultrasound, I was getting excited. My brother wanted a baby brother, but I wanted a baby sister. The doctor asked my mom if she wanted to know the baby's gender and my mom said, "Yes."

"It's a.... girl!" The doctor said. I was so happy, but my brother wasn't. My brother started crying. More months went by, and I was at school. My dad picked up my brothers and me early from school. I asked my dad where we were going, but he didn't say. We then arrived at the hospital, and we went into a room that my mom was in. She was holding my baby sister. I was so excited. My mom then let me hold my sister. I was overcome with excitement. That day I will always remember.

This changed my life, because I finally had someone to play with me and I never felt lonely anymore. This was a moment that matter to me.

Did you ever wish for something? And how did it change life for you?

JILLIAN'S

MOMENT

MOMENTS MATTER

Jillian Blackwell

Did you ever think that you could ever end up with a rare disease? Well I did, but I never thought that I would. And what I had; believe me when I say, you never want to have. This is what happened:

One day sometime close to me going to first grade, I woke up with a tingly feeling in my face. I thought it was the feeling you get when you wake up and want to go back to sleep. I got out of bed and went to the bathroom. After I brushed my teeth and washed my face, the tingly feeling was still there. So I looked in the mirror. I saw bumps on my cheeks, lips and my nose. My lips were a red color standing out from my light brown skin. I told my mom and she made an appointment for me to see the doctor a few days later. By then, I had broken out in a full blown rash all over my face. It was itchy, peeling and it was red where the bumps were. The doctor gave me some medicine to use on my face and told me to come back in two weeks.

School started right after that. Even though I was using the medicine the doctor gave me to use, my face was still peeling, itchy and red. So I couldn't concentrate in class. Although I wanted to do my work, I needed to scratch my face. And although I wanted to make friends, everyone avoided me.

But I did meet my best friend. I can't tell you her name, but I can tell you that she is still my BFF today. When we went back to see the doctor, she told us that I had a rare disease called, 'Perelfacildermatitus.' I was shocked, and she told me that it would get better. And she was right. Today, people say that I am pretty and that they can't see my bumps. I know they are still there, but I am happy with them and I love myself just the way I am.

JULIE'S

MOMENT

MOMENTS MATTER

Julie Robinson.

The moment that mattered the most to me in my life was when my niece was born. The date was May 30th 2015 when a beautiful loving baby was born named, Natalia. She was such a joyful little girl, who brings a smile to so many people's faces. I never would have thought I would've met such a caring little girl that could change my life. I remember hoping one day I would have someone to call my baby sister or brother. Instead I got a loving caring, joyful, niece that I would be happy to call and treat like my little sister any day.

I remember the first time I got to see and hold her. She was so small and was so adorable. When I held her I felt so happy, and she made me so joyful inside. It was an amazing moment to see her in my arms. The moment was priceless and something I would never forget. It was an amazing day. I will always cherish that moment, because it means a lot to me. It means a lot to me, because that's the day I got what I can call a mini me; something I always wanted.

She is joyful. Because every time I see her, she has the biggest brightest smile on her face that can lighten up a room. She is caring. Because every time she sees a person that doesn't look happy she will ask them, ''Are you okay?" and tries to make people have a good time and smile. She is loving, because she cares for others. She has such a soft heart and everyone loves her.

I love to see her. She brightens up my world and all the other people around her. I love to run around and play with her; she is very energetic. She loves to play with others and explore. She is a little explorer *in* the making. She loves to see what things are and touches a lot of things she is very interested in.

I want to make sure she is very successful when she grows up and is able to be independent. I want to teach her how to read, write, spell, count and much more. I want her to not just learn from me from what I know, but also from the other people in her life as well. I want her to be able to listen to what people have to say and take it in to consideration. I want her to listen to what other people have to say. Because there are a lot of good people in the world that know what they are talking about, that can help her become even more successful in life. I want her to know she can be and do whatever she wants as long as she puts her mind to it.

I want her to be the best she can be. I will be there to help her along the way to make sure she becomes as successful as possible. She can talk to me when she need too. She doesn't have to be afraid to talk to me. I want her to know I am and always will be there for her.

I feel that it is important for me to be a role model for her, because I want her to see how I handle certain things that I have to go through in life. I want her to know what to do when there are different situation and how to handle them. I want her to know there are a lot of bad things going on today in the world, but there are many good things in the world as well. No matter what the bad is there's always a good side to the problem and or situation. I want her to be a successful young lady and always know that no matter if the problem or situation is good or bad, I will always be here for her through whatever.

SOPHIA'S

MOMENT

Sophia Do

The moment that mattered to me the most was on the last day of elementary; I was graduating from fifth grade. As you could imagine, everyone was in tears. It was truly one of the best days ever to me, and I finally got something I've been wanting for so long. We got food, and we also got to spend time with some friends and family. It was amazing. I'll start from the beginning.

I got up that morning, and it was a bright day. I was so excited for this day; well it *was* the last day of school after all. I got up to go brush my teeth, and my sister was already at school like always since she was a sophomore in high school. After I finished in bathroom, I went to my bedroom to see what clothes she laid down for me. It was a teal dress. The top was teal while the bottom was striped zigzag with white and teal. It also had a little jacket; which of course, was teal as well. Teal was my favorite color, but I thought there was maybe a little *too* much teal. I put it on, and started to worry if people would think that there was too much of one color, but it was too late now. I ate breakfast, I went off to school, and my mom was driving.

When we finally arrived, I went straight towards my classroom. All the chairs were arranged in a circle. I looked around the room to see everyone wearing something fancy; except for my friend, who was wearing a shirt and pants. She always refuses to wear dresses. I sat down next to her. We talked for a while until it was time to go. Our school has a church right next door to us, and the church owners agreed to let us borrow the church for the assembly. We went up the stairs of the church, like we practiced. We were all in order;

shortest to tallest. We sat down at our seats we were assigned to. I saw all the people below us, since we were on a semi-balcony. I saw my mom come in, but she sat way in the back. The graduation music started to play, which was are cue to go.

We started to go down the stairs, in the order we were supposed to go. Then, we went down the aisle, one by one. When it was my turn, I walked down between the pillars. It was so tense. I finally reached my seat, and sat down. I looked around the room. The church was huge. There were about five chandeliers and so many rows of seats. There was a small alter in the front middle of the room. The teachers let everyone get settled in first, and then some other music started playing. It was a song about growing up. It was pretty sad, and the adults already started tearing up. During the song, five kids went up to the altar holding signs. It seemed that it was a kid from each grade: kindergarten, first, second, third, fourth and fifth grade. Yep, growing up. The song soon ended. Our principal and assistant principal went up to the altar to say a few words in the microphone to all the parents. After that, we all stood up and started to sing "Stand in the Light," by Jordan Smith. I could see that a lot of adults started recording us, and they were streaming even more tears. When the song was over, we all sat back down and about everybody clapped. Then, someone from one of my friend's class went up to the microphone with some lined paper in their hand. They were reading some good memories they had when they were in elementary. Eventually more people came up and started reading theirs, too. Finally, it was time to get our certificates for graduating. We lined up, and one by one went up the altar. When it was my turn, I walked up. My teacher handed my certificate to me, and I shook all the teachers' hands. I then went and sat back down. We had to place our certificates under our chairs, so we wouldn't get tempted. After all the classes went, it was time. There were going to be a principal's award trophy to a certain *three* people! My principal was on the altar, ready to say the names.

"And the first principal award goes to... Sophia! Come up and get your award!"

I was super surprised, I honestly didn't expect that. This was super important to me, because this was my first time *ever* getting a trophy. I gladly went up, and everyone was clapping. I got my trophy, and I was told to stay up there. So I just stood there smiling awkwardly. Then, my friend from another class got called up for a trophy too! She was also running up and smiling. When she got her trophy, she had to do the same as me – stand there holding the trophy.

Then the last guy got called up. We all stood there for a moment so all the parents could get some pictures. Next, we got off the stage and went back to our seats. I started to inspect the trophy a little more. It was a black board, with a big golden star at the center. At the bottom, there was a plaque with my name on it, and under my name it said "principal award." I put the trophy down.

Then, they started projecting something on the white board. It was a little film from us then, to now. Basically there were baby pictures of us we brought in, and then it showed a picture of us in a graduation garments from picture day. When each picture of a baby popped up, everyone would try to guess who it was. I'm pretty sure that everyone guessed that my baby picture was me when it showed up on the board. All I could hear were people yelling my name when my picture came up. At the end; before the graduation celebration was over, we got up and sang one more song. We all sang, "God Bless the USA." After that, we were all dismissed.

We had one more room for celebration. It had lots of foods and snacks. I was with my mom and friends, and we went in the building. There were also a lot of picture booths. My friends and I went into one. We then sat down at a table, and got some sour punch. We also got some cupcakes and ate them; even though, I'm not really a big fan of cupcakes. I opened the pack, and there were a bunch of certificates and a quick recall medal for being in second place in our match. Yes, I was in quick recall, and so were my friends. After a while, we all left.

I would have to say, I had a blast at the graduation. If I could live it over again, I definitely would. I did get two new awards, after all. I got to eat some snacks and be with my friends and family. I had loads of fun. And this is; and will always be, a memory that I will remember. Always do your best, even if you don't like to. Most of the time, you will be awarded for your hard work.

WILLIAM'S MOMENT

MOMENTS MATTER

A Scary Moment That Mattered To ME

By: William Monroe

My dad drove me back to my Mom's house after we watched a scary movie. My 18 year old step sister was the only person home, and she was fast asleep. I grabbed my towel and proceeded to take my shower. After showering, I walked down stairs to my room with my towel around my waist. While I changed into my night clothes, I heard something fall from the other room. When I got my shirt on, I tip toed to the other room. When I turned on the lights, I saw my younger sister's doll lying on the ground. Her other dolls sat straight up on her bed just looking at me. I stood still in her room silently staring at the dolls for about 20 seconds. Then I turned off the lights and went back to my room.

Now I am even more scared.

"It's scary enough that my room is in the basement, but why does there have to be dolls?" I said to myself.

I heard the washing machine turn on, "OH CRAP," I said as I jumped in my bed and pulled the blanket over my head. A few minutes later, I pressed play on the movie ghost busters until I fell asleep.

I begin to dream vividly. In my dream, it was dark but I noticed light that appeared to come from the moon. I felt myself running not knowing why, and realized I was in a forest. I heard foot steps behind me! 'Wait what was that?' I stopped. I heard heavy breathing. Every time the person or whatever it was exhaled, I heard a crackle in its breath. I tried running again, but I couldn't. It felt like my power had been drained away from me. I can't believe

I'm saying this, but I felt inferior to it and I didn't even know what it was.

I looked down and realized now that I was in quick sand. "What THE HECK", I said as I struggled to move my feet.

I looked up, and I saw the most terrifying thing ever. I could tell it was a guy but it looked like a monster.

As he stared into my soul he said, "Hello boy. My name is Orochi Maru."

"What are you?" I said.

"Well, I'm the demi god of death. But since I'm the demi god, I only eat kids. Now you die," he said.

But then, the sand consumed me and put me in a shell that got rock solid. Trapped, I took my dagger and stabbed a hole through the shell. Then I blacked out. When I came to, I saw that I was in a cave. I saw the stalagmites and stalactites surrounding me. I had never been so scared. I again passed out.

I then awoke to my mother yelling for me to get up. That's when I realized that a scary movie had made my normal environment seem even scarier, which then caused me to even to have a nightmare. This moment mattered to me, because it appears scary plus scary equals scarier. Never again!

WIZDOM'S

MOMENT

Wizdom's Moment

Ever since I was little, I played alone; like a single leaf flying through the early fall air. But in my mind I longed for a sibling; preferring a sister, but a brother would do as well. Hoping my siblings would be as playful as my puppy that slept **all** the time. As I grew up alone still longing for someone to call my sister or brother, I gave my hopes up on having playmate for life.   And then as I was watching TV, my mom walked up to me. I started to think I is was in trouble not knowing what for. As she sat down, I was becoming worried thinking I was in big trouble. She gave me the news, **'I was going to have a sibling.'**   I was so excited then I asked, "Is it a boy or a girl?" She said, "Well we don't know yet."

After hearing the news I started to think, 'Were they going to be as playful as I imagined? Would they be loving and caring? 'Would they even want to spend time with me? A few months into my mom's pregnancy, she could figure out what the gender was. I wanted to go with my mom to her appointment to figure out the gender, but sadly I was not allowed. So I went to school working as hard as I could trying not to bear the thought of what could possibly change my life forever. Later on in the day; unexpectedly, a soft sounding older lady's voice came over the intercom to tell my teacher that my parents were here to pick me up. As she said this I thought, 'The question I have been asking myself may be answered.' I rushed down the hall way trying my best not to get in trouble. Finally after what felt like was a marathon to the office door was right in front of me. I hesitated to open the door knowing what was behind it would change my life forever.

The silence on the way to the car was torture. We finally got to the car with them walking slower than a snail. I finally just shouted out, "**What is it?**" They just started laughing then they said, It...........is...............a............boy!" I was so excited on the outside; but on the inside, I truly felt upset. The sister I imagined was no longer able to exist; only in my thoughts, but this perfect sister would never exist because it was a brother. A brother was what I had to look forward to. I had to deal with it. So I helped my mom prepare for the new baby. I helped her move her room around, so the baby could sleep in her room. I was her feet and hands to run errands and lift. Everything was preparing for the new baby. The house I once knew was no longer. It would now be baby friendly.

Finally the time came. The sibling I longed for, for years would soon arrive. I had to wait hours in the waiting room, because I was not allowed to be in the delivery room. My stepdad came out of the room to the waiting room, and told me that I could come see mom and the new baby. I finally came in to see my mom and new brother. In spite of everything, I walked into the room and immediately fell in love with this little baby boy I didn't even want. I asked if I could hold him but his dad said, "No." So when his dad went to the restroom, my mom let me hold him. He was so small sweet and cute. As he got older, he became my whole world, and I can't imagine a life without him in it. His birth was a major moment that mattered in my life, but each day with my brother is a treasured moment for a lifetime.

www.ingramcontent.com/pod-product-compliance
Lightning Source LLC
Chambersburg PA
CBHW071137250626
47159CB00006B/2245